The Teachings of Babaji

Compiled by

Vladimir Antonov,
Ph.D. (in biology)

Translated from Russian by
Mikhail Nikolenko
Ph.D. (in physics)

Corrector of the English translation —
Keenan Murphy

2007

ISBN 978-1438212760

Babaji is one of the well-known Divine Teachers of humanity, a Representative of the Creator.

He taught (and continues to teach us now — from His non-incarnate state) how we can walk the Path to Perfection, to cognition of God, to realization of the purpose of our lives.

From this book we can learn what He told people during His last Divine Incarnation on the Earth.

The book is intended for all people.

Contents

www.swami-center.org
www.godteachesus.org
www.philosophy-of-religion.org.ua

Preface

This book presents to the readers the Teachings about the Path to spiritual Perfection by Avatar Babaji from Haidakhan (India).

Babaji is the One Who of His Own Will incarnates on the Earth from age to age to help seekers of the Truth and to edify the spiritual leaders of our planet.

One of the earthly lives of Babaji is known to us from the book of Yogananda[1]. Yogananda describes, among other things, how Babaji easily dematerialized and then materialized again His body, when He wanted to move to somewhere on the surface of the Earth. He also performed materialization of objects.

The next coming of Babaji to the Earth in a body was from 1970 to 1984, again in India (He materialized a body that was already adult). He taught people the art of the highest steps of the meditative practice and advised His followers on how to organize their lives better in front of God.

This is a reduced version of the title Teachings of Babaji (published by "Haidakhandi Samaj", India,

---

[1] Yogananda — Autobiography of a Yogi. "The Philosophical Library", N.Y., 1946.

1990). The original consists of the introduction and a selection of all recorded sayings of Babaji presented in chronological order, including sayings addressed to concrete interlocutors only. For this edition, only those statements of the Great Guru were selected which are of significance for all people and in all times.

The Teachings of Babaji

You should seek harmony in everything that you do!

We must shed all jealousy and envy, because they are harmful.

There will always be hills and mountains to overcome on the way to God. ... It is the duty of warriors to move the mountains!

(In the ashram) all people are prohibited from distributing food, clothes or money to the villagers. This creates an atmosphere of expectation and when it is not met, then the people return to steal things from the ashram.

All who come to the ashram must take responsibility for its care.

You must consider work as the real devotion.

Do your duty! Do not be idle! This is an age of action! Perform your Karma Yoga! Show ideal actions to the world! Service to humanity is service to God and worship of God!

Everyone should forget nationality: we are one here! This is a universal family! Have no idea of separation of identity: discard feelings of separateness! Serve the people with mind, body, wealth, and knowledge!

We are all equal, independent of the country we come from, and national differences should be ignored! We are all a unity!

Work as a unit: there is no caste or creed here, there are no differences!

Babaji blesses all who do their duty sincerely and with devotion! Do your duty lovingly!

Whenever the world faces the most difficult problems, the Lord takes on a human incarnation and comes to fulfill the needs and desires of humankind. However, when the Lord comes in human form, few recognize Him. Only those to whom the Lord wishes to reveal Himself realize that He is in fact more than just a normal human.

You may think that Babaji just sits here doing nothing. But He has been everywhere and is everywhere! He is doing much! Babaji sitting here is still present in the hearts of everyone in the world!

Those physically distant from here should not think they are far away — they are equally close to Me!

I do not recognize castes and races! I behold only one humanity! I am working for mankind while here!

Kindle the light in yourself, then kindle it in others! Like spreading light by lighting one candle from another all around a room, — so we should spread love from heart to heart!

If you are worthy, I shall show you freedom greater than the one you have dreamed about!

To become strong does not mean to become harsh and heartless. To become strong means to grow beyond pleasure and pain, beyond heat and cold!

There is no saint without a past and no sinner without a future!

There are many doctrines. Adhere to one principle — that of Truth, Simplicity, and Love. Live in truth, simplicity, and love and practice Karma Yoga!

I have come to guide humanity to a higher Path. I do not belong to any particular religion, but respect all religions. I seek the elevation of all mankind.

The result of hard work is happiness and the result of laziness is pain.

I want you to become brave warriors and attend carefully to your own duties! This is good for you!

Now a change on a vast scale, like those at the time of the Mahabharata, will take place.

Do not fall back in your work but go on! Karma Yoga is your first duty!

Every moment, in each breath, while eating, sleeping and working, remember the Lord!

Even the Sun and the Moon can move from their course, but the faith of a devotee should not be shaken! Never be moved by false doctrines!

While your minds and hearts are impure, how can God live in your hearts? The water to clean the heart is the name of God. So, teach everyone to repeat the name of God — everywhere.

I do not want idle people! Japa[2] does not take the place of karma[3]! Japa and work go together!

I do not want japa to be a pretext for idleness! Do japa with your work and be liberated!

Work and be the Light; repeat God's name!

Attachment to material things makes man cling to life[4]. While you are attached to life and afraid of death, you die with that fear and that weight clinging to you. If you die without fear and remembering the name of God, then the soul leaves the body free of that fear and attachment. If you are reborn, your soul is still free from that fear. If you die in Unity[5], you are free from rebirth, unless you will it.

We must always have good thoughts for each other!

All of you must be happy and healthy! Appreciate the joy of life!

The seeds of righteousness have been sown in your hearts for you to kindle the hearts of others! I seek the general good of all people in the world!

---

[2] Repetition of names of God.

[3] Here: action, work.

[4] To life in the body, to the body.

[5] In Unity with the Divine Consciousness.

You must do everything that is possible to perfect humankind! All people will be saved if kindness and mercy will prevail. You must work to elevate humanity and eradicate pride, jealousy, and hatred. Unite in love to elevate yourselves! Each one of you must vow today to sacrifice everything to obtain (such) Oneness!

Be rid of attachment! And be prepared to burn your very bones, if necessary, to secure the public good and righteousness.

Why do you attach your minds to the transitory things in this world? Attach yourself to God!

Remove hatred and jealousy from the heart! The same thing was taught by Jesus Christ. Where there is jealousy and hatred, there is no religion!

I dislike idleness and gossiping! You have taken this birth on the Earth to work. Work hard! After death, what will you show to God? Not only here, but wherever you are, work hard!

Don't use intoxicating drugs but learn devotion and purity. It is strictly forbidden to use drugs! If you do so, there is no progress, you remain the same!

All of you must learn to be disciplined. Be alert 24 hours a day! All must vow to work and serve always, think good and do good! According to My plan, Liberation will come only to those who practice Karma Yoga.

Whatever money comes to you, spend it for good purposes!

I say all this in the service of humanity. To work, think good, and dedicate your life to humanity is the best! Each corner of the world must awaken to these words!

Only hard work can make a person powerful and energetic!

Think good! — Be good! — Do good! One can follow any religion, one can follow any practice or path, but one must be humane!

You should sing devotional music in a way that stirs the soul — it should evoke deep feelings. You should sing with love! Do not sing like you are taking part in a theatrical performance! When you make music, it should touch the heart so that it leaves a memory on the mind! When you sing, you and those who listen to the kirtan[6] should enjoy it! It (kirtan) should be sung in harmony, with a slow rhythm. Put the soul into it, and it will flow! The melody should flow in all its sweetness!

Think of the Earth as of a Mother! This is one Earth! Don't be divided by thinking of yourselves as belonging to different countries! We belong to one Earth! Look to the future with a vision of good deeds for the whole world, not just one country!

When human beings come in this world, they forget their duty and fall into the attachment of maya[7] and into the concepts of "me" and "mine", and so they forget God.

---

[6] Public worship with a chanting of names of God.

[7] Illusion.

Jealousy and hatred are the two causes by which humanity is ruined. In your lives these two vices should have no place!

I am against non-violence that makes a human being a coward. Fight for Truth! To face life, you must have great courage every day!

Everyone must be courageous, facing the difficulties of life with bravery! Cowardly people are like dead people!

I want to create a world of brave people who face life as it comes!

Keeping this basic principle in mind, our main duty should be to spread the Message of Karma Yoga in the world. We ourselves give an example to all, by practicing it!

Service to humanity is the best service to God! Our motto is "work is worship"!

The only way to obtain siddhis, to become really strong, is karma — action.

If you learn right action, you can do anything! Action is Mahayoga — the Highest Yoga! You should progress through action! Man is meant for action!

The main order of Mahaprabhuji[8] is that you must be punctual in all your duties, always!

There are many kinds of Yoga, but Karma Yoga is of supreme importance! Karma Yoga must come first, and then others types of Yoga can be added.

---

[8] By this name Babaji sometimes called Himself.

The great people who lived in the past thrived by doing Karma Yoga!

Karma Yoga teaches you to live a true life! Only Karma Yoga is able to transform the world. Inaction is the cause of pain and all troubles!

Train your children in Karma Yoga, so that they may become people of good and strong character!

Take care of the body! As long as the body is in good health, you can serve! When you are sick, how can you serve? It is very important to have good health! In order to do karma, it is vital to keep your body healthy! So, follow these teachings about cleanliness and health and teach others, also!

So, all of you have to go beyond the fear of death and the hope of life and go on doing Karma Yoga! We must perform those actions which will benefit others — and not only other people but the whole of Creation!

Shri Mahaprabhuji wants a world of very brave and courageous people! If, with full faith and devotion to God and with a firm determination, people follow the Path of Truth, Simplicity, and Love with Karma Yoga, they will reach their goal! When the whole world is burning with the fire of sins and sorrows and the flames are about to swallow the world, this is the only way by which humanity can be saved!

There must be no place for fear! People must work fearlessly in the world! When man is fearless, no one can stand against him in battle — either a battle in material life or in spiritual life! He is victorious in all the battles of life!

Mahaprabhuji has control over the "god of death".

Mahaprabhuji can create many worlds and can destroy many creations at His Will. If you are His devotee or disciple, why should there be any fear in you? You should not worry at all! Be fearless!

Now Babaji is suggesting another point — that we must annihilate the feelings of "I-ness" and "my-ness" from our minds. When you all belong to this whole universe, where is the place for "I" and "mine?" By this means only will the world be benefited. This is not the concern of one individual but that of the whole universe.

Everyone must remove the differences between themselves and others and work in the world in unity!

There is only one way for mankind to be saved and that is by changing the hearts of all people. Shri Mahaprabhuji will give His full Spiritual Power to this, but every man and woman will also have to make their best efforts towards this end!

In every way, in every manner possible, do good to others and make them happy! To each individual and to every country, provide what they lack!

If you are engaged in doing good deeds and go on doing good acts, you will have good sleep, good appetite and bad thoughts will not cross your mind. Otherwise, you will always be criticizing others.

The food which we eat must be clean and nutritious. We should pay special attention to everyone's health! Wherever there are centers, people should try to grow and cook good vegetables and make halvah and distribute them to others. Food should be nutritious so your strength for working will increase and your minds will be strong, too. It is necessary to keep the body in good health in order to do good karma! If the body is not strong, how will you work? We should eat nutritious food so our bodies become energetic and our brains work better[9]!

I want a world of strong and healthy people! I want people in this Creation to be as fast in their actions as the wind! I want people who work with all their bodily energies! At this time, the world needs such brave, strong people!

We must follow a Path which will strengthen us! How can that be done? It can only be done when you are hard working and active! That is why it is very essential to be active and hard working! See Babaji here, Who is working from morning until evening like a machine!

We must depend on ourselves and not lay our burden on others!

No one should cease the practice of Karma Yoga! This is the eternal, unshakable Way!

---

[9] Nutrition in the ashram of Babaji, as in all other truly spiritual religious schools, was purely killing-free (i.e. excluding any meals made of meat or fish).

The fact is, a great fire of sins and sorrows is burning throughout the world. Everyone living walks and works through this fire! Death is dancing before everyone's eyes!

The calamities, which are coming to this world, are unavoidable. Only the one who has a strong determination to do good acts and who is strongly devoted to God can survive this destruction!

Only the one who has surrendered completely to the will of God is secure!

You should not do anything which will do harm to others. Only that work which benefits the majority of people is truly called Karma Yoga.

I tell you that you must all spend your time and energy working for the good of the entire universe! Only by doing this will you be benefited! Whatever we do, we will ourselves to do, must be based on the universal good!

You must all step together and form a great international organization — bigger than anything organized in the history of the world!

We must advance for the sake of upliftment of humanity!

We have to go beyond the hope of life and the fear of death! Whatever happens, we must go ahead! You should not be afraid of fire or water! When the need arises, we will have to jump into the Ocean! When the time comes, we must be prepared to jump into the Fire! That is why all of you must be firm and stable! You must have only one aim, one goal — to serve every living being in the universe!

Only those who are very alert and careful can be successful in their lives!

I do not like dishonesty! I want everyone to be honest and dutiful!

Everyone must do their duty correctly! You must know what you should do and be busy doing it. By karma one will not fall but will always rise higher! No work is low or bad in this world if it is done in the right spirit!

The leaders should be those who are very able, who are full of all virtues and capable of spreading this Message. There must be weight and wisdom in their words, so people would like to obey them. A leader must be selfless, one who desires to work for the upliftment of humanity! The leaders must be dedicated to their country and spend all the time for its upliftment. They must be able to encourage people. It is very important!

Everyone must use their own common sense and do their duties without waiting to be told what to do. To do your duty is the greatest worship (of God), the greatest service, the greatest devotion and penance (tapas)!

You must seek Liberation and help others to achieve Liberation!

Babaji's Formula

(This chapter is reprinted from the book of Vladimir Antonov 'Ecopsychology' [5])

We have already examined all stages of the spiritual Path in the terms of Patanjali's scheme. Now let us discuss the same problem using analysis of the formula of spiritual development suggested by the Avatar Babaji. This formula sounds as follows:

Truth — Simplicity — Love — Karma Yoga (Service to humanity) — Abandonment of the lower "I" for the sake of merging with the Higher "I" of God.

* * *

The advent of Jesus Christ — a Messenger of God-the-Father — had been prophesied by numerous Jewish prophets. But when Jesus did come — only some of the Jews acknowledged Him as Christ; those were the people who became His first disciples and spreaders of the Teachings of God, which were new for that region of the Earth. But the official Synagogue never accepted Jesus as a Messenger of God-the-Father and... for almost two thousand years has been waiting for another Christ...

A similar phenomenon happened in the near past: all mass organizations calling themselves

Christians did not recognize God Who appeared before people of the Earth in the human form!

Jesus Christ Himself prophesied: "When you see One Who was not born of a woman, fall on your faces and worship. That One is your Father" (Gospel of Thomas, 16; see [14]). In 1970 Avatar Babaji came to the Earth exactly in this way — but "Christians" did not recognize Him.

(Now another Avatar — Sathya Sai Baba — works on the Earth, preaching the same Eternal Universal Teachings of God-the-Father — and again the hierarchs of all mass Christian confessions refuse to recognize Him!).

God became a competitor to many religious organizations: for He can "entice away" their "flock" to Himself. Who would then support all those for whom Churches are a source of income? This is why some "parsons" intimidates the congregation: "everything that comes from the East — is of Satan!", or "if you do not stick to us, you will surely go to hell!"…

But Jesus Christ was embodied in the Middle East — in Judaea. Krishna, Babaji and Sathya Sai Baba — all of Them are from the East. So, is God — "from the East"?

* * *

Babaji is One of the Representatives of God-the-Father, a Part of Him. He periodically embodies on the Earth as an Avatar in order to help people. One of His incarnations took place at the end of the 19th century; it was described by Yogananda [16]. The next one was from 1970 to 1984 — again in Northern India, where He appeared before people by materializing a body of a young man for Himself, in which He lived for 14 years.

Now Babaji, together with Jesus Christ, Sathya Sai Baba, Krishna, and other Divine Teachers, Who are Manifestations of God-the-Father, keeps on helping worthy disciples of God — but this time from the non-embodied state.

From His last incarnation on the Earth Babaji left people a concise and brilliant version of the Teachings of God, the "core" of which is the mentioned above short and exhaustive list of what we, people, have to accomplish. The main thing for us now is to try to understand correctly what these words mean and then to fulfill all this.

Truth

This part of Babaji's formula implies understanding what God and the Evolution of the Universal Consciousness are, what our place in it is, and what exactly we have to do. Today almost everyone lacks this understanding.

In India at present, the favorite "folk's god" is fictious Ganesha: a man with an elephant's head, who was allegedly born in Heavens of copulation of other "gods".

In "Christian" world people sincerely believe that their God is Jesus Christ and that Muslims have another God — false, of course, — Allah, although Allah is simply a translation of the term *God-the-Father* into Arabic language. And it is love for Him and aspiration for Him that Jesus Christ preached.

At present most "Christians" have lost both God-the-Father, Who was preached by Jesus, and LOVE, which is essential for attaining the Creator...

This is why any intelligent person has to learn to see the difference between true *Christianity* as the *Teachings of Jesus Christ* — and those interpretations of them that exist under the same name. And among the latter, one may single out various degrees of distortion up to its absolute perversion, to its antithesis.

What have to do those who consider themselves Christians? They have to study the Teachings of Jesus Christ and follow them!

To make realization of this task easier, the Teachings have to be systematized on the considered subjects [4] and there must be a methodology of their realization [4-6].

* * *

Some readers may think: the author is criticizing everybody — maybe he wants to present himself as a "Savior"?

No, I want to present as a Savior not me but God! I need neither fame nor popularity: I chose a modest and quiet monastic life for myself. I want to help people. And I serve God.

... Yes, God does not lead infidels to Himself by the Straight Path. These are the words from the Quran.

And the Straight Path to Him is the Path of Love: love for people, for all living beings, for the Creation and the Creator. This is the Path to Him as the correctly understood Goal. This is the Path of purging oneself as a soul of everything that is not Divine: including coarseness, violence and all kinds of egocentrism — and of replacing self-centeredness with God-centeredness. And all of this is real!

If you could embrace non-incarnate Jesus Christ Who appears in a human-like form and feel His Divine love, Subtlety, and Tenderness — combined with unlimited Power resulting from Unity with the Universal Consciousness of the highest eon, and Divine Wisdom — then you would realize right away what God appreciates in people and what He wants us to be like.

But in order for us to be honored with such an Embrace, we have to get closer to Him — not physically but by the characteristics of the soul.

* * *

One of the ways to answer the question "What is the Truth?" is:

"There is Evolution going on within the Body of the Absolute.

"Our Goal is the Creator. Our task is to transform ourselves from a part of the Absolute into a part of the Creator, to enrich Him with ourselves.

"In order to fulfill this task we have to become Love — strong, wise, and refined to the level of the Primordial Consciousness."

Simplicity

Simplicity means sensible naturalness of the way of life and behavior, as well as modesty and lack of arrogance and self-importance. Simplicity is a pre-requisite of Love. It is also an indispensable tool of spiritual warriors, which God wants us to be.

The best way to develop simplicity is to keep close to nature and to learn how to attune to its harmony. Here, in the solitude of forests, fields and lakes, without make-up on the face, earrings, fancy synthetic clothes or even with no clothes at all — we can love the beauty of the Creation and the Creator, accepting help from God in the optimal way, expanding with the consciousness in the beauty of the Creation and in the Holy Spirit.

Simplicity is also beautiful in expressing our love for other people: in a smile, friendliness, tenderness and openness with friends.

But it is important to know the limits. For instance, walking naked among those who do not understand you and propagating your understanding of "simplicity" in this way — this is tactlessness; this cannot be called a harmonious and spiritual action.

The same principle can be applied to sexual relations: the "simplicity" that results in sexually transmitted diseases and unwanted pregnancies, as well as that, which is connected with violence and selfishness — is not what God wants from us.

"Spontaneity" in expressing and realizing all of the whims, needs and desires, which is encouraged in some modern pseudo-spiritual sects and other organizations, also does not have anything to do with the true Simplicity.

Only the Simplicity of intelligent people who belong to the sattva guna and of those who have reached even higher spiritual heights is the true Simplicity.

People of the tamas guna understand simplicity as either sugariness or violence, rudeness, scuffle, and lying drunk in the mud.

The true Simplicity is one of the elements of the "training for God". It is not for those who are far from Him.

Love

Love is the main quality of God. In order to merge with Him (or even to escape hell, to begin with) we have to learn to feel emotions of love and to perform deeds of love, to eliminate all the opposite states and actions, whatever circumstances we may live in.

Love is the main thing that God wants from us. And we do not have any other possibility to cognize Him and to merge with Him, unless we transform ourselves into Love.

Love is a special emotional state; in other words — this is a state of the energy of the consciousness. And the consciousness (soul) is what every one of us is in reality.

Every time we leave the state of love, we alienate ourselves from God. "Every instance of leaving the state of love results in accumulation of bad karma" — this is what God told me once [8].

People blame their misfortunes and diseases on anyone but themselves. Although it is always they who are to blame.

It is of paramount importance for us to understand that the stable and confident state of love can be achieved only through practicing special psychic self-regulation techniques, which must include working with the chakras, primarily with the anahata chakra. (We describe these methods in the book [5]).

In the ancient Christianity a special method of "opening" the spiritual heart was developed, which got named Jesus Prayer. Adepts had to repeat constantly a special prayerful appeal to Jesus, and after years of practice some of them succeeded in making the prayer "break through" into their spiritual hearts — and this made them realize what love really is. When this happens, the whole life of such a person changes dramatically [15].

… Once God, seeing my sincere aspiration to Him and my strong desire to help people, helped me create a tremendously efficient system of methods of "opening" and development of the spiritual heart. Some of these methods were described in several books of mine and were widely taught in Russia and some other countries some time ago.

However, I need to mention that out of thousands of students, only a few were able to attain the actual and quite complete cognition of God-the-Father. What was the reason for the "dropping out" of the rest? It was their inability to thoroughly comprehend the points of the *Babaji's formula*.

The overwhelming majority of the students were lacking that intensive aspiration for cognition of God, which could allow them to switch their attention to Him from the objects of the material world. Others gave in to threats of sectarians.

The psychic techniques per se cannot make a person attain God; they can only play the role of wonderful and necessary aids. But the main prerequisite of success is the ability of the spiritual seeker to comprehend with the developed intellect the entirety of the Truth and to build a steadfast loving aspiration for the main Goal, in other words — to fall in love with the Creator.

The true spiritual Path necessarily implies the complex development of a person, which must include intellectual, ethic, and psycho-energetic components.

Also, a person cannot successfully cultivate real love only by performing exercises with the anahata chakra during meditation classes. Development of love must fill one's whole life and pervade all of his or her activities.

It must be manifested:

— in staying constantly with the concentration of the consciousness in the anahata chakra,

— in sincere respectful and tactful attitude towards everyone, whether one knows them or not,

— in the ability to forgive and forget insults quickly, without taking revenge,

— in behavior that excludes any possibility to offend or aggrieve someone wrongly.

Love has to include a sacrificial component of willingness to help others even if it goes to one's own detriment. Interests of those who deserve this help has to be given a higher priority than one's own.

Love must be directed not only towards God and people, but also towards animals and plants; nobody may think that their love is developed if they are still able to kill or maim plants unnecessarily, if they allow themselves to eat bodies of animals for the sake of satisfying their gluttony.

Love has to be irreproachable in relationships with children. This implies being incapable of getting irritated. Although, being demanding in teaching children discipline and honesty should not be excluded — in the interests of the children, in the first place!

Everyone should analyze the characteristics of their love in the sexual sphere, since this is where human vices usually are manifested very vividly.

Any kinds of violence or constraint in sex — even in the verbal form or in thought — are examples of a behavior opposite to love.

Carelessness of a man as to the prevention of unwanted pregnancy is another example of the same type of behavior.

Passiveness of a woman during a sexual intercourse when she is not aiming to give her love to her male partner, but only selfishly expects satisfaction for herself, being able to resent him for doing something "wrong" — is a phenomenon of the same nature. (Since all people differ by the features of their sexuality, and the new partner never knows in advance how to satisfy you better!).

True sexuality is the art of giving yourself and your love to the partner through sexual relations. And only a combination of sincere and giving love on the side of both partners can make such relations harmonious.

I am sure that many women would benefit from reading the wonderful book of Barbara Keesling [11], which promotes the practice for women of giving their sexual love as a gift. Although I would not recommend doing everything that is written there. For example, practicing oral sex regularly increases the risk of transmitting infections dramatically. Also, sexual relations with so many partners are absolutely incompatible with a serious spiritual Path: during a sexual intercourse an intensive energy exchange takes place between partners, which results in taking on possible energetic coarseness, impurities and diseases of the partner.

... Everyone builds their destiny themselves, using the freedom of will granted to us by God.

Someone develops in sacrificial love by helping others. Someone cultivates capricious egotism, hatred, coarseness, cruelty. The former forbear and forgive, do not become immersed in hostility and thus preserve themselves in love and aspiration for the Creator — and attain Him. The latter become "refuse of the Evolution". The former can be truly called Christians. And the latter, though wearing crosses and visiting churches, — how should one call them?

Our sexuality was conceived by God not only as a means of reproduction but also as a method of spiritual development. It facilitates the cultivation of such aspects of love as tenderness, care, self-giving, merging of two consciousnesses into one, which prepares one to the Mergence with the Consciousness of the Supreme Beloved — the Creator. Sexual love can directly contribute to the development of the spiritual heart, which we have already discussed. It also teaches us Peace (if everything goes well), which is an indispensable component of Perfection, one of the qualities of God, which we need to master.

But all this relates only to the sattvic, pure sexuality of people who make real progress on the spiritual Path. In this case it does accelerate their advancement significantly.

But sexuality of coarse and egoistic people who do not possess developed spiritual hearts can be disgusting and bring them to hell.

The spreading of a perverted "Christianity" that has lost love became a damnation for the spiritual evolution of many people of the Earth. Among other things, it pronounced anathema against sexual love and declared renunciation of it a "Christian feat". It profaned all conceptions by calling them "defiled" as opposed to the "immaculate" (i.e. without a man) conception of the mother of Jesus Christ that allegedly took place. The human body itself, especially the female body, was declared shameful. In the past, "decent" people felt shy to say even the word *legs*. The words that related to the sexual theme were declared "indecent" and transformed into cursing — a means of defiling other people. In this way the obscene language was created — the language of the tamas guna.

And how could a pure attitude to sexuality form in people who regard it as an odious "vice", who hate sexuality in themselves and especially in others? But without this pure attitude towards sexuality one can hardly succeed in refinement of the consciousness, development of love, and getting close to God.

People started to fear what in reality could help them to become better!

Many men came to hate women exactly for what women could help them with. Since women are, in general, significantly more refined than men, if for no other reason than their hormonal status. And by this characteristic they are closer to God.

Jesus Christ taught the same [14] in addressing men:

"Respect her, uphold her. In acting thus you will win her love and will find favor in the sight of God...

"In the same way, love your wives and respect them...

"Be lenient towards a woman. Her love ennobles man, softens his hardened heart, tames the brute in him, and makes of him a lamb.

"The wife and the mother are the inappreciable treasures given unto you by God. They are the fairest ornaments of existence....

"Therefore I say unto you, after God your best thoughts should belong to the women and the wives, woman being for you the temple wherein you will obtain the most easily perfect happiness. Imbue yourselves in this temple with moral strength. Here you will forget your sorrows and your failures, and you will recover the lost energy necessary to enable you to help your neighbor.

"Do not expose her to humiliation. In acting thus you would humiliate yourselves and lose the sentiment of love, without which nothing exists here below.

"Protect your wife, in order that she may protect you and all your family. All that you do for your wife, your mother, for a widow or another woman in distress, you will have done unto your God." (Life of Saint Issa, 12:13-21)

But "Christianity" (and not only "Christianity")... declared woman... "the source of sin" and prescribed to cover her body in any possible way.

In Russia for many centuries women had to wear special long dresses when bathing and even to sleep in clothes: "What if you die in your sleep — you will appear before the Lord naked! What a shame it will be!".

Another example of a similar kind of abomination is declaring some children "illegitimate" and holding up to shame the motherhood of these women to whom God entrusted the upbringing of these children!

… We need to understand that it is people of the tamas guna who are immersed in vice and who do not see anything except it, while possessing aggressiveness, seize the "reins of government" in the originally holy religious movements and gradually turn them around to the opposite direction, warping the doctrine of God to its exact antithesis.

In the sexual aspect of life they — while themselves belonging to hell, obsessed with passion for violence, defilement, and satisfaction of their egoistic lust — are unable to imagine that for other people, sattvic ones, sexuality does not mean lust, but a way of sharing their love, giving it to other people as a gift and that this may be their way of serving God!

* * *

But getting obsessed with sex is also not good. The term fornication is valid not only for people but also for God. It denotes both too many sexual contacts and sex with inadequate partners (those who are not at the same level of the spiritual advancement). Sexually transmitted diseases are the mechanism that God uses for slowing down the tendencies for sexual amusements in people.

The truth here is that we have to try to direct all our attention towards searching for God, without distracting ourselves excessively for anything else. (And sex is just one of such distractions).

… So, in sex, like in everything else, everyone has to find the golden mean between two extremes…

* * *

Refinement of the consciousness and true sattva, as a necessary stage of cognition of the Holy Spirit and God-the-Father, are impossible to achieve without accepting and understanding concepts of BEAUTY.

"Beauty: Cosmos establishes Evolution on this formula" — this is what God taught us through Helena Roerich [11-12].

Spiritual beauty exists at two levels of the scale of gunas: rajas and sattva.

Rajas is, in particular, boldness, self-discipline, and beauty of exploit. It is manifested in a spiritual warrior with unbending will.

Rajas can be found in the states of nature; it also can be expressed in dancing, music and fine art. Examples of the latter are paintings of Nicholas Roerich.

Sattva — spiritual purity and beauty, refined and saturated with tender love — is the last step on the stairway leading to cognition of the Holy Spirit.

In nature we can observe sattvic states in the purity of sunlight at dawn, in singing of spring birds, in charming silence of a tranquil evening, etc.

Among the most vivid examples of highly sattvic music are some compositions of Ananda Shankar.

Sattvic beauty of harmonious human body is also spiritual and can attune the one who observes it to tenderness, tranquility, and peace, which so many of us are lacking.

* * *

And another comment on the subject of love.

One day I was traveling by train, perfecting lowliness of mind when studying the situation: among my fellow travelers were a mother and a son. She had a huge body and was very rude. Her son — a military cadet — was about fifteen years old. All the way she constantly shouted. About what? It… was just her regular manner of talking to her son, shouting everything that was coming to her mind: all her thoughts. For example: "Darling! I am going to go to the toilet and throw out the apple core!… Why don't you answer, when your mother is talking to you???!!!" And her exhausted son was looking at the window with a dull expression on his face being only able to nod listlessly…

How can the behavior of this "mommy", who sincerely loved her child, be characterized?

Was it violent? — Yes, it was. Was it tactless? — Yes, it was. One could name some more of her traits… But what is important to stress now is that her love lacked peace.

The ability to feel deep inner peace, especially when there is no need to perform energetic actions is a very important and valuable quality. It is a fundamental prerequisite of true love.

Attempts to love without this inner peace sometimes turn into what I have just described. Such "love" can only cripple its victims. It induces in them only an urgent need to escape. If there is a place to escape to…

… The state of God-the-Father in His Abode can be described as Tender Peace. Let us learn this from Him when preparing ourselves to meeting Him.

But true peace is not something opposite to a sound drive and energy, but matches them harmoniously. Let us analyze this postulate — and apply it to our lives!

Karma Yoga (Selfless Service)

The term Karma Yoga means "Path to Mergence with God through performing selfless service".

What is *service to God*?

An incompetent reader may start to recall: "I know the term *Divine service*... What is it? Prayers... And what are prayers? 'Lord, give me this! Lord, give me that!'"...

Yes, for the majority of believers who consider themselves Christians, praying means begging something from God. And, paradoxically enough, they see in this their duty and their "service to God"...

But God does not need our panhandling! He does not listen to it! Otherwise it would "make Him sick" to hear all the nonsense that people invented, their addressing Him as a servant who is allegedly supposed to supply whatever He is asked for.

He needs our efforts on self-development and our help to other people in this. He wants us — every one of us! — to take an active part in His Evolution, rather than to whine passively and expect "grace" from Heaven...

Helping other people on this Path — this is what service to God is! He declared this through Jesus Christ, Babaji, and Sathya Sai Baba; the apostle Paul said many wonderful words about this as well [4].

But one should not interpret this kind of help too narrowly: only as preaching, conducting religious classes or writing religious books. No. In order to live on the Earth fruitfully and to evolve, people also need housing, food, clothing, fuel, transport, safety, medical help, education and many other things. Therefore, Karma Yoga means helping other people in everything that is good.

The most important characteristic of Karma Yoga is the right motivation: that is, one should not act for gain or reward, even in the form of a salary. One has to perform actions for the sake of helping other people, as acts of selfless giving. This does not imply, however, an unpaid work. But it is up to those whom we help and to God to take care of the material welfare of the giver.

In other words, the essence of "mutual settlements" of worthy people who help one another is exchange of gifts. All necessary details of the "theory of giving" are set out by God in chapter 17 of the Bhagavad Gita [4].

The essence of it is that God regards only those gifts as sattvic, i.e. true and pure, that one gives to a worthy person at the right time and in the right place.

So, the short definition of the term *Karma Yoga* sounds like this — "selfless help to all worthy people in everything good".

It is very important to emphasize that one develops correctly not through parasitism, panhandling or endless repetition of prayers or making ritual bodily movements — but through creative work and active love for other evolving beings, which is expressed in actions for their good.

Sathya Sai Baba clarifies the idea of Karma Yoga by the following illustrative example. He says that if you are members of one family you do not ask the head of the family for payment for each kind of work you perform around the house — it is outside people that work for money, but not the own ones. So you, if you feel that God is your Father, you must not engage in bargaining with Him, but on the contrary — you must act in the interests of His Plan, for Him, for the Evolution and not for your personal gain [4].

This kind of activity is the background against which God allows us to develop intellectually, in love and in power.

Abandonment of the Lower "I" for the Sake of Merging with the Higher "I"

This is the final part of the Teachings of Babaji. It includes Mergence of the individual consciousness of a person who has reached the highest eon with the Consciousness of the Creator. At that, the person's self-awareness dissolves in the Ocean of the Creator.

Attempts of the leaders of some sects either to destroy fully the self-awareness of their disciples without providing them with a new substrate for self-identification[10] or to convince them that they are already God should be regarded as incompetent and extremely harmful. One's self-awareness

---

[10] Sometimes leaders do this on purpose — to make slaves-zombies from their disciples.

must not be destroyed but transferred. And the cognition of God and Mergence with Him are not performed through being convinced or convincing oneself, but by means of stage-by-stage penetration with correctly developing consciousness into more subtle eons, their exploration, establishing in them, mastering Mergence with the Consciousness of the Holy Spirit first and then with the Consciousness of the Creator. All other directions prove to be dead-end and lead to either delays in the person's development or to cultivation of gross vices and turning to the direction opposite from God, which is fraught with diabolization and insanity.

Work on this part of Babaji's formula should begin with elementary correction of one's behavior in communicating with other people.

For example, the tendency of many people to dominate over others, to behave as if they are the "boss", to look "important", — looks comical from the standpoint of spiritual growth.

Violence, resentfulness, jealousy, revengefulness, wrathfulness, desire to *own* people and things (except for essential ones), sexual desire, like any intensive wanting of something from people or from God, — all of these are vicious manifestations of the lower "I". They must be eliminated.

Jesus Christ and His Apostles left many invaluable formulas-precepts for us: do not sit at the high place, if you want to grow spiritually — become a servant to other people, never resent or revenge yourself, regard others as higher than yourself, etc. [4].

Lao Tse and Juan Matus were saying about exactly the same in a very straightforward and concise way [4][11].

It takes deep self-analysis and hard work on repentance in order to get rid forever of manifestations of the "protruding" lower "I".

We have to understand that there is no such phenomenon as "forgiveness of sins" whatsoever: God does not have such a concept.

The purpose of repentance is not obtaining forgiveness for concrete acts that we have done, but getting rid of vices.

"Sins", i.e. our mistakes, are either consequences of our lack of experience and knowledge or specific manifestations of those qualities of our souls that are called vices.

The true mechanisms of deliverance from vices are self-analysis, repentance, and strict self-control.

If it is not possible to eliminate the vice that has been discovered and realized right away, one should recall the entire line of its manifestations — starting from childhood (and sometimes from the previous incarnations). And one has to re-experience anew mentally all situations, which one previously resolved incorrectly, but this time in

---

[11] In order to understand correctly the works of Carlos Castaneda, one has to read the book of his wife Margaret Castaneda [10].

---

the right way. Moreover, it makes sense to "play over" in advance all possible future situations when this vice can manifest again.

It is also important to try, if possible, "to redress the wrong" to those whom we harmed — be they people, animals or even plants. Even if they are not currently "alive" on the Earth — we should address them as non-embodied souls. And let us remember that God really accepts such efforts on getting rid of our vices.

We need to repent of all the instances when our non-love for other people and for God was manifested, as well as of all our egoistic actions and emotions.

* * *

Many dull-egoistic persons try to push their bodies into a subway train car as soon as the doors open without letting the people get out first.

Or, while waiting for a bus or a tram, they block the sidewalk with their bodies, instead of standing on the side so as not to hinder anyone from passing by, thus showing care for other people.

Or, entering the subway station hall some people hold the spring door behind them to help the following person get in, while others let the door go, crashing their "neighbor" with it.

Even when they get into a sound spiritual school, egoistic primitive people behave in the same manner. As long as the course is conducted, they feel good; they are happy and filled with bliss. But once the course is over — they start to feel bad: they have already gotten used to the situation when someone is making them feel good; and suddenly it stops… And since they do not feel good anymore, they start to experience increasing negative emotions towards the instructor and the school…

Egoistic people know only their selfish interests and resent when an obstacle in the form of someone else's need gets in the way of their satisfaction.

When a person strongly wants something from anyone, it is an indication of the viciously protruding lower "I" of the one who wants. This triggers the mechanism of bio-energetic "vampirism" and becomes the cause of diseases of those, from whom a person wants something [8], and of "aggravation" of destiny of the one who wants.

But loving people are always being attentive and care not to hinder anyone in anything, but, on the contrary, use any possibility to help everybody, giving the interests of other people a higher priority than their own.

Such people are always polite and benevolent, strive never to offend anyone without a reason, even when not in the best states, being sick or tired, for instance.

In sexual relations they never obtrude themselves but wait for the moment when the partner desires the same.

... In this kind of self-analysis, detailed recommendations by Sathya Sai Baba can be of great help [4].

* * *

When we have achieved the deliverance from coarse emotional states and the ability to attune to sattvic phenomena of life, this allows us to begin with meditations of "dissolving" ourselves in harmony of the surrounding space. Such meditations can be especially effective in quiet evenings, at dusk — in the forest, prairies, at lakesides, seashores, or near other water bodies. The meditation should be performed using the following formula: "There is only harmony of the surroundings: forest, lake, — but there is no me". At that, the consciousness expands from the anahata chakra and merges with the subtlety and purity of nature.

The next fundamental stage will be mergence with the Holy Spirit in Pranava meditation (see below), and then stage-by-stage mastering of the total reciprocity (Nirodhi) in the eons of the Holy Spirit and God-the-Father.

This is how man completes the personal evolution forever, becoming a Part of the Primordial Consciousness, a Part of the Creator. After that such a soul continues to live creatively — not as a separate being but as Him.

Conversations with Babaji

"Babaji, tell us please how did You become Divine?"

"Since the time when the Himalayas rose up — Babaji has been on the Earth. I became One with the Ocean of the Creator so long ago that I feel Myself as Eternal as He is. I cannot even remember that in the past I was a separate soul.

"Do you know, for what purpose the Avatars come to the Earth? They come to reestablish the link between man and God, to manifest on the Earth the reality of God, to remind people who they are and why they are here...

"Avatars come when the light in souls and righteousness in lives of people fade, when people look only at the world of matter and do not want to know anything more.

"From age to age, I come to the Earth!

"I manifest Myself so that one can touch Me with one's hands and not be burned...

"I speak so that My words can be heard by many and spread throughout the Earth, and thus people may remember that there is God...

"I restore the Eternal Law of God...

"I work miracles to make people know that I am not a small body but God — the Creator of the manifested universe...

"Yet, the most important of everything I do is the change of the direction of souls' growth:

"from darkness — to Light,

"from fear — to fearlessness,

"from hatred — to love,

"from wanting for *oneself* — to giving to others,

"from laziness and sleep of the soul — to *Karma Yoga*, that is selfless service to God through serving people.

"Every Avatar does this.

"Be heirs to My art of redirecting souls, 'smelting' them in the *Divine Fire* in order to rid them of vices and evil, growing them so that their hearts bloom with Love for God!"

"Babaji, how can one learn not to leave the state of Mergence with You?"

"One has to become the *Ocean!* One has to perceive oneself as the *Ocean* — the *Ocean* where there is only Babaji!

"Babaji means Father!

"With the arms stretched in Me and from within Me one has to caress, support, heal!

"One has to feel oneself as an integral, inseparable Part of the Whole, coessential to the entire Primordial Consciousness! Then no power in the world of matter can separate you from Me!

"In general, everything goes well! No one expected such a quick success from you! We supported, helped you, but did not expect that you would manage to 'break through' all together!"

＊ ＊ ＊

Once we were walking on a wonderful *place of power,* where one can always meet Babaji. Vladimir and others, gathering mushrooms, went forward, and I stayed for a minute to embrace Babaji...

"Don't fall behind, follow him: *your babaji!* He is a Great Master equal to Me!"

"Babaji, do You know what he said a moment ago? He said that he has not mastered yet the siddhis demonstrated by You, like the control over matter..."

"I know!" Babaji smiled radiantly, embracing all of us with His Love — me and Vladimir with his friends walking through the beautiful *Dale of Babaji.* "Of course, I know it! But I know also that he would not exchange the great art of *transforming souls* mastered by him for any kind of siddhis like materializing smells or making objects disappear..."

＊ ＊ ＊

"Having students does not make one a Master...

"Possessing knowledge and meditative methods is not enough for leading people to Me.

"One has to learn to love them as I love!

"The miracle of love is in its selflessness and, as a result, in the absence of wanting something from others.

"Love is that 'foundation' which can help you to solve 'troublesome' situations. Only love — as a thing completely devoid of egoism — can show you the way out of the 'thicket' of problems born by the ego (lower self).

"When in you there remains nothing but love, there are also no problems, by which the lower self torments itself.

"All negative emotional states result from the attachment of the lower self to earthly affairs.

"Everyone goes through life situations where his or her lower self gets manifested — until it is erased completely.

"If you act consciously in such situations — you can reach success quite quickly.

"Success here means that, having cognized Me and merged with Me, you do not exit from Me — in any circumstance.

"Learn to look at earthly affairs with the eyes of God!"

"Is it You Who supervises Russia now?"

"Yes. I also care about everyone worthy of it, including you."

"How are the duties distributed between You and other Representatives of the Creator?"

"Every One of Us has Their own fields of activity in Divine Service depending on the personal developments in the past. Someone protects, cherishes, educates children. Another supervises those engaged in sports. Others, including Me, provide help on the Path of cognizing the Highest and spreading the higher knowledge.

"As you know, Every One of Us has something to share. Thus We serve, first of all, with the highest abilities We have.

"Every One of Us has a favorite work. I am One of Those Who help you directly, in any moment of your lives. And I stretch My hand towards any appeal if it originates from you or your friends.

"I know about all your affairs. And I never forget about the needs of every one of you!

"Every One of Us exerts every effort so that the School may grow and the situation may develop well!

"From every one of you I expect maximal efforts for fulfilling the Plan which I designed for creating a spiritual Revolution on the Earth — *Mahakranti*."

* * *

"Everyone who crosses the last border on the spiritual Path comes to the *Full Freedom*. Yet, crossing this border requires one's desires and aspirations to be directed to *My World* — the *World of My Freedom!*

"People's desires and aspirations can be likened to ropes that either bind one to the world of matter or help one to move to the other side of the border.

"I will help everyone worthy! Yet, until they stretch their 'ropes' across the border to My side, while they are attached by the 'ropes' to their side — they can hardly cross the border.

"I live for you: for all those who are worthy of this!

"And you, the worthy ones, must repeat My Path!

"Only those who assume this obligation are guided by Me along the Path towards Me, towards the Unity with Me and with all of Us!

"If, on the other hand, egocentrism prevails in a person, then let this person develop himself or herself without My help! I have nothing to do with this!"

* * *

"I give you everything you want. I realize your desires. But only when you stop desiring — only then My Will can be realized through you in fullness!

"… I want to talk once more about love and sacrifice.

"If you have no love which is ready to sacrifice itself in service to Me — I cannot accept you in Myself! In such a case, you cannot merge with Me, become Me! For I am the Sacrificial Love!

"I am also Wisdom! If you waste your love, you will not be able to achieve Mergence with Me!

"To be ready for Calvary does not mean shouting about the Truth everywhere — and being killed then! It implies that you are ready to give all of your life — to Service to Me and to the Path to Me!

"Let your love be guided to realization of it by My Will!"

＊ ＊ ＊

"Your School is for those who want to come to Me, only to Me! It is for those who have chosen Me as their Highest Goal and do not thirst for anything else!

"Let others seek their own ways. They, too, will come to Me but not now.

"Your path is straight like a flight of an arrow. And you must not offer this path to those who seek now only earthly well-being and happiness. They have other paths.

"Remember this always and do not offer your path to those who do not want to walk it *up to the end!* In the past, you had other directions from Me, but they were needed for your own development.

"And one more thing: to want and to try to go *to the end* as much as you can does not mean that you will reach the end in the current earthly life. But it is this desire — to exert all your efforts out of love for God! — that is the main criterion here!

"... Wide distribution of knowledge usually results in perversion of the original Teachings. Therefore when an Avatar comes to the Earth with a Divine Mission, He or She brings to people Dharma — the Law of God — in its original purity. An Avatar does not bring psycho-techniques intended for achieving Perfection in Mergence with God. Realization of the Straight Path is always the task of esoteric schools, schools for the chosen.

"Avatars prepare the soil for Divine sprouts. They redirect large masses of people of the tamas guna from hatred and inane activity — to love and righteousness. But the real spiritual sprouts will appear only in the next incarnations of these souls.

"The task of schools of the Straight Path consists in helping a few students chosen by Me. It consists also in giving to people pure knowledge about the Straight Path.

"The Straight Path is like an elevator shaft leading to Me, to My Abode! It is a *secret passage*. If it becomes available to unworthy people, then I close it and destroy such a situation completely.

"Look: even the methods for opening the anahata are an accelerated technique! And it is not always good to give to a person very quickly the knowledge which he or she would have to master, in normal conditions, during the entire life!

"This can be likened to a situation when one comes to the mountains on a helicopter instead of walking afoot for many days through swamps and brooks, with a heavy backpack, cold nights, wet feet, yet with beautiful sunrises and sunsets, through beautiful valleys. One appears at the same place in the end, but without the experience that can be gained from walking the path afoot!

"Moreover, if one does not want or is not able to go further to the mountains, overcoming glaciers and precipices, in order to reach the summits — then this indicates that such a person is not mature enough.

"… Consider the following example: if a teacher in a regular school with an undeveloped anahata tried to give this knowledge to students, then how many children — because of this bad teaching — would dislike the knowledge which they would otherwise like! You may recall the despise you felt towards some books that were imposed on you in the school!...

"... Successful opening of the anahata signifies the beginning of the Straight Path to God! Yet even in this task you should not help everyone! Only they deserve practical help in this matter who make their own efforts on the path of mastering love.

"It makes no sense to give to people answers to the questions that have not arisen in them yet! And one should not teach even the most remarkable methods to those who are not burning yet with the desire to love Me and to cognize Me!

"You have to leave for the next generations only 'beacons', pointers on the Path, which will help seekers of Me find Me, not more. These are books and films about love for nature, about the meaning of life and the methodology of its realization, also photographs. This is what I need from you!

"... For small children there are one set of rules, for adults there are others. For children there are rules of the game where kind God rebukes them mildly, corrects them, and always forgives them... As for adults, they have to strive to live according to the Laws of My Beingness — the Laws of Love! And if you do not observe these Laws, they will turn against you and the entrance to Me will be closed for you for centuries...

"At the stage of mastering Mergence with Me, the control over your states of the consciousness does not work automatically. This control depends entirely on you! But the Laws mentioned above still have their effect here! And no tears or promises, like 'I will never do it again!', can influence these Laws.

"The essence of My Laws is Love! Not the love which you receive, but the love which you give to others, to Me!

"Any of your deeds performed not in the state of love can result in your fall. By betraying the state of love, you betray Me!

"To become Me, having merged into Me, means, among other things, to become Love for all creatures and to love everyone infinitely, as I do!

"Those who do not understand this rule or disregard it are not allowed to come to Me; I do not allow it for their own good.

"… The process of transformation of the personal self into the Higher Self is hard. It cannot happen at once just due to the fact that you understand its necessity. One has to transform oneself into Love! And for this purpose one needs constant self-control and self-correction!

"But when it happens — then truly Great Happiness comes: you enter the highest form of being — Being Me!"

The Head Wind

*I send the head wind to those who
have chosen the Straight Path.
It is not for weak souls!*

The head wind blows away the ashes
and ignites the heart!
I am sending this wind! I am going towards you!
Do not yield to weakness and fear,
do not seek the ways of escaping!
I am embracing you with My Heart
and dissolving your pain and doubts!
I am hugging you with the Fire
of My Love and Power —
And the scraps of your ego burn down
like old useless rags!
I am taking off the shackles from your heart —
Surrender to My Divine Power!
This is how ore is purged of slag
and becomes pure gold.
Become the purity equal to Me, become —
only Me!
Love will merge with Love,
and I will become you!
I will make My feet your feet!
With My words I will fill your mouth!
With My Love I will fill your heart!
And let your Path on the Earth become Mine!

* * *

"Let nothing but Me remain in You! Then your karma from the past will be washed away completely! You are standing at the threshold of the future and looking into it with My Eyes! It is the great *now* in Mergence with Me! My Hands show you the Way, My Love illuminates the Heaven of the eternal beingness!

"I am everywhere! I am in every creature. I live and work on the Earth in every one of you. Through your bodies, let My intentions be realized!

"I am the Father and the Mother of everyone. Become united with My Love!

"I am the Higher Self of every one of you!

"I am looking in your future: it is clean! I guide — through you — all worthy ones to the final Victory: to Mergence with the Infinite Consciousness of the Creator!

"The word *God* sounds differently in different languages, but in all developed spiritual hearts *Love* sounds the same! All people of the Earth have to come to know this, with your help in particular.

"I want to say so much to people through you!… Nirvana, Nirodhi is My Path… And let many embodied people walk these steps through you! This is the purpose of the work that you do on the Internet. One has to make available to mankind a serious foundation of spiritual knowledge! Relate this knowledge with My name! And when this knowledge begins to spread on the Earth as a powerful wave — only then the river of worthy souls will flow into the Ocean of Me!"

Bibliography

1. Antonov V.V. — The New Upanishad: Structure and Cognition of the Absolute. "Polus", Saint Petersburg, 1999 *(in Russian)*.
2. Antonov V.V. (ed.) — Spiritual Heart: the Path to the Creator (Poems-Meditations and Revelations). "Reality", Saint Petersburg, 2003 *(in Russian)*.
3. Antonov V.V. (ed.) — How God Can Be Cognized. Book 2. Autobiographies of God's Disciples. "Vilna Ukraina", Lvov, 2005 *(in Russian)*.
4. Antonov V.V. (ed.) — Classics of Spiritual Philosophy and the Present. "New Atlanteans", Bancroft, 2008.
5. Antonov V.V. — Ecopsychology. "New Atlanteans", Bancroft, 2008.
6. Antonov V.V. (ed.) — Forest Lectures on the Highest Yoga. "New Atlanteans", Bancroft, 2008.
7. Antonov V.V. — Spiritual Heart — Religion of Unity. "New Atlanteans", Bancroft, 2008.
8. Antonov V.V. — How God Can Be Cognized. Autobiography of a Scientist Who Studied God. "New Atlanteans", Bancroft, 2009.
9. Antonov V.V. — Sexology. "New Atlanteans", Bancroft, 2009.

10. Castaneda, Margaret — A Magical Journey with Carlos Castaneda. "Myth", Kr., 1998 *(in Russian)*.
11. Keesling Barbara — Healing Sex. "Piter", Saint Petersburg, 1997 *(in Russian)*.
12. Klyuchnikova M.Y. (compil.) — Living Ethics. "Respublika", Moscow, 1992 *(in Russian)*.
13. Shyam R. — I Am Harmony. A Book about Babaji. "Peace Through Culture" Association, Moscow, 1992 *(in Russian)*.
14. The Life of Saint Issa: Best of the Sons of Men, In: Around Jesus, "Society for Vedic Culture", Kiev, 1993 *(in Russian)*.
15. The Way of a Pilgrim, Kazan', 1911.
16. Yogananda — Autobiography of a Yogi. "The Philosophical Library", N.Y., 1946.

Our video films:

1. Immersion into Harmony of Nature. The Way to Paradise. (Slideshow), 90 minutes (on CD or DVD).
2. Spiritual Heart. 70 minutes (on DVD).
3. Sattva (Harmony, Purity). 60 minutes (on DVD).
4. Sattva of Mists. 75 minutes (on DVD).
5. Sattva of Spring. 90 minutes (on DVD).
6. Art of Being Happy. 42 minutes (on DVD).
7. Keys to the Secrets of Life. Achievement of Immortality. 38 minutes (on DVD).
8. Bhakti Yoga. 47 minutes (on DVD).
9. Kriya Yoga. 40 minutes (on DVD).
10. Ecopsychology. 60 minutes (on DVD).

11. Yoga of Krishna. 80 minutes (on DVD).
12. Yoga of Buddhism. 130 minutes (on DVD).
13. Taoist Yoga. 91 minutes (on DVD).
14. Ashtanga Yoga. 60 minutes (on DVD).
15. Agni Yoga. 76 minutes (on DVD).
16. Yoga of Sathya Sai Baba. 100 minutes (on DVD).
17. Yoga of Pythagoras. 75 minutes (on DVD).
18. Psychical Self-Regulation. 112 minutes (on DVD).

You may order our books at Lulu e-store:
http://stores.lulu.com/spiritualheart
and at Amazon:
http://astore.amazon.com/spiritual-art-20

You can also download for free our video films, screensavers, printable calendars, etc. from the site:
www.spiritual-art.info

See on the site www.swami-center.org our books, photo gallery, and other materials in different languages.

Our other websites:

www.philosophy-of-religion.org.ua
www.teachings-of-jesus-christ.org
www.pythagoras.name
www.atlantis-and-atlanteans.org
www.path-to-tao.info

www.new-ecopsychology.org
www.encyclopedia-of-religion.org
www.meaning-of-life.tv
www.highest-yoga.info

Design by
Ekaterina Smirnova.

Become acquainted with photos
of this Great Divine Guru:

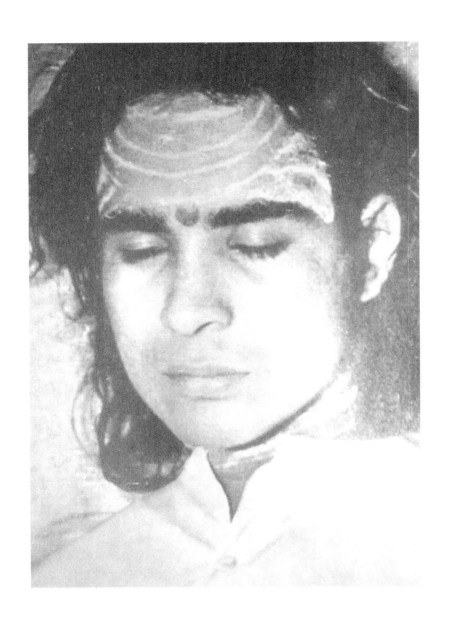

Printed in Great Britain
by Amazon